# THE
## TAO
### OF

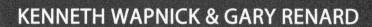

# KENNETH WAPNICK & GARY RENARD

The Interactive Companion Journal to
the film featuring wisdom from
Kenneth Wapnick, Gary Renard
& iKE ALLEN

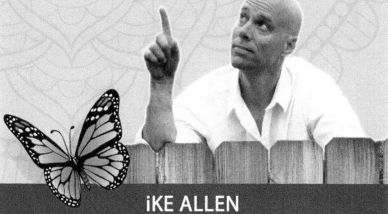

# iKE ALLEN

A paperback original

Cover & Book design by iKE ALLEN

Book layout by Ande Anderson, MS, RD

Printed in the United States of America

10 9 8 7 6 5 4 3 2 1

AVAIYA
A Limited Liability Company
6397 Glenmoor Road
Boulder, CO 80303
www.AVAIYA.com

# CONTENTS

# A MESSAGE ABOUT KEN & GARY FROM ENLIGHTENMENT VISIONARY, iKE ALLEN

My life is filled with Miracles. I coach people and lead seminars around the world about helping people wake up from the dream while still playing within it, and in my spare time, create films and books, too. Over the years, I've had the great privilege of working with many extraordinary people committed to enlightenment.

Two of my films, *A Course in Miracles THE MOVIE* and *Leap! A Quantum Awakening*, feature Kenneth Wapnick and Gary Renard.

While creating supportive resources I've had multiple opportunities to spend time with Ken and Gary.

The three of us have always lovingly and playfully shared our insights on Enlightenment from Buddhism to *A Course in Miracles*.

Did you know there is an A Course in Miracles TV channel? Learn more at www.ACIMTVNETWORK.com

8

This inspired me to create a new film and companion book that would blend our wisdom to help support people on their journey.

This book is a rich tapestry of multiple interviews over the years from Ken and Gary blended with insights and action steps from myself.

One of the most amazing parts of the book, *A Course in Miracles*, is that it specifically states that "a universal theology is impossible, but a universal experience is not only possible but necessary." It emphasizes that it is but one version of the universal curriculum. There are many others, this one differing from them only in form. They all lead to God in the end.

As most spiritual practices promote that their model has the truth, it has been refreshing to explore *A Course in Miracles* knowing that it clearly states it is only one of many versions of the universal curriculum. Ken, Gary and mySELF have all studied a plethora of different paths throughout our lives and I believe this is part of what has

Did you know there is an A Course in Miracles TV channel? Learn more at www.ACIMTVNETWORK.com

allowed us to be relatable to so many people.

This powerfully loving book, *The Tao of Kenneth Wapnick and Gary Renard* is designed to accelerate your awakening by combining our wisdom and experience with non dualistic philosophies like Taoism and *A Course in Miracles*. In addition it is designed for you to become a co-author with us embracing Helen Schucman's actual technique of Scribing in this book.

Helen Schucman, a Professor at Columbia University, scribed (channeled) *A Course in Miracles* via conversations with Jesus. The voice made no sound, but seemed to be giving her a kind of rapid, inner dictation which she took down in a shorthand notebook.

Ken, Gary and I are highlighted for a moment of each day, and then you have the opportunity to accelerate your own spiritual journey with journaling and/or practicing scribing in the accompanying pages.

10

I hope you find this material beneficial in your journey to the other side of the bridge.

You can additionally see Ken, Gary and myself featured in many other films, books and courses, available at www.avaiya.com/ACIM. Kenneth Wapnick passed away on December 27, 2013.

To fully benefit from this version of *The Tao of Kenneth Wapnick and Gary Renard* please journal each day. It is not a task, but a wonderful opportunity to truly learn more about yourself, Ken, Gary, myself and actual enlightenment. If you miss a day, simply pick up where you left off last.

**Digital Ebook Readers:** If you're reading a digital version of this book, it may allow you to type directly into the document. If not, many ereaders like iPads, Android Tablets, Kindle Fire, etc., provide access to apps that you can journal in. Please search your app store or search to find one that works for you.

Did you know there is an A Course in Miracles TV channel? Learn more at www.ACIMTVNETWORK.com

11

You can also go to www.AVAIYA.com to share your experiences and read about others on their journey. I hope you find joy, Inspiration and wisdom from this book and your journaling.

Did you know there is an A Course in Miracles TV channel? Learn more at www.ACIMTVNETWORK.com

12

**This extraordinary book belongs to:**

_____

You are about to co-author your own book with Kenneth Wapnick, Gary Renard & iKE ALLEN, by journaling in these pages.

Please list the three things you would most like to experience while you read and journal in *The Tao of Kenneth Wapnick and Gary Renard* (It could be as simple as choosing three of these: Awakening, Joy, Passion, Love, Inspiration, Gratitude, Integrity, Prosperity, Freedom, Hope, Health, Appreciation, Enlightenment).

To fully benefit from this book, please list three now before turning the page:

1. _____

2. _____

3. _____

Did you know there is an A Course in Miracles TV channel? Learn more at www.ACIMTVNETWORK.com

# WEEK 1

## The Illusion of Separation

**The iKE ALLEN Tao Series**

*Our experience is that we're bodies, that we're separate, that we live in a dualistic world. So what we need to do is figure out how to change that. Albert Einstein said that a person's experience is kind of like an optical delusion of consciousness. So we look out there, we see all of this separation. It's actually what the Hindus would call the world of multiplicity. And it's not true. But we think that it is true. It doesn't do us any good to deny that this is our experience. Our experience is that we're here and that we're in these bodies. What we want to do is figure out a way to change that experience from the experience that we're here in these bodies, to what we are and where we really are. And the fastest way to do that is to change our interpretation of that which we are seeing.*

**~ Gary Renard**

**"Enlightenment is but a recognition, not a change at all."**
-*A Course in Miracles*

Day 1: Most of us know the Albert Einstein quote, "Reality is merely an illusion, albeit a very persistent one." If The Course quote above is true, would anything change for you if Enlightenment came knocking at your door? Would there still be a you? For me, nothing changed and everything changed. I still play the character of iKE ALLEN, but my awareness is Oneness. Before Enlightenment, chop wood, carry water. After Enlightenment, raise the thermostat and turn on the faucet. Today, journal about Enlightenment. Not what The Course says, what Buddha says, etc. Journal or Scribe from within you. -**iKE**

_____

_____

_____

_____

_____

_____

_____

_____

_____

_____

Did you know there is an A Course in Miracles TV channel? Learn more at www.ACIMTVNETWORK.com

*You have two parts to the mind. You have the conscious mind, and people think that the conscious mind is real important. They think it's what you think and what you see with your conscious mind that runs you. But that's not true. What really runs you is the part of the mind that you can't see, the part of your mind that's hidden from you. It's like this ocean of unconscious mind that's underneath the surface. And hidden there is a lot of crap, there's a lot of deep ontological unconscious guilt that people aren't aware of. But that's what really runs the world. That's what's responsible for all the madness that we see on our television screens, all the war, the crime, violence and disease, all the separation, compulsions and addiction-driven behaviors that we see, it's all being driven by this stuff that is in the unconscious mind that we can't see.* ~**Gary Renard**

17

**"The Kingdom of Heaven *is* you."** -*A Course in Miracles*

Day 2: What if you gave up preserving the integrity of your individual self? If The Kingdom of Heaven is you, what would happen? Open to Holy Spirit today and share below in your journal.

**-iKE**

_____

_____

_____

_____

_____

_____

_____

_____

_____

_____

_____

_____

_____

Did you know there is an A Course in Miracles TV channel? Learn more at www.ACIMTVNETWORK.com

*All of our illusions can be traced all the way back to the original idea of being separate from our source, and the tremendous amount of guilt that accompanied it on this massive metaphysical level. In order to escape from it, we had incredible denial and projection outward. So now all this stuff that was in the mind appears to be outside of the mind. It appears to be outside us and really there, when the truth is that all we're seeing is a symbol of that which exists in our own unconscious mind. Now if you put that together with the fact that there's really only one of us, and of course a modern physicist would confirm that, that once you get down to the subatomic level you can't really separate one thing from something else, everything is one, whole, connected. If you put those two ideas together then you start to realize that if what you're seeing is a symbol of what's in your own unconscious mind and if everything is really one, then what are we doing if we go through life judging and condemning other people? ~ **Gary Renard***

19

"You are not the victim of the world you see because you invented it." -*A Course in Miracles*

Day 3: I live my life in the knowing that this world came and went long ago and yet, there is still an experience here of and "I" and that "I" has children, friends, clothes, money, etc. How do you believe your life would occur if you were "Right Minded" all the time? If you truly understood their is only ONE? Do you still believe you would judge the "others?" -**iKE**

_____

_____

_____

_____

_____

_____

_____

_____

_____

_____

_____

Did you know there is an A Course in Miracles TV channel? Learn more at www.ACIMTVNETWORK.com

*Without realizing it, all that we're really doing is judging and condemning ourselves. It may look like we're directing it out there but there really isn't any out there. It's really just a projection. It's a projection of a universe of time and space. And the way to undo that projection - which is the equivalent of undoing the ego when it comes to Buddhism - the way to undo it is through change in your interpretation of that which you are seeing. Because by doing so you're actually changing your interpretation of yourself. So as a quick example, let's say I'm driving down the highway and somebody cuts me off in traffic. And I say "Oh that son of a bitch!" Well I just called myself a son of a bitch without realizing it. Because there's not really anybody out there for it to go to because there's really only one of us and that one appears as many. It's the Hindu's world of multiplicity. You have one appearing as many.* ~ **Gary Renard**

**"All things work together for good."** - *A Course in Miracles*

Day 4: Are you still fighting against forces outside of you? Do you question Gary's words? My words? The ACIM quotes? Take a few minutes to focus on what it means to simply be a Mind. Afterward, share your thoughts in your journal or simply put pen to paper and discover what you write. **-iKE**

_____

_____

_____

_____

_____

_____

_____

_____

_____

_____

_____

_____

_____

_____

Did you know there is an A Course in Miracles TV channel? Learn more at www.ACIMTVNETWORK.com

*There's just one ego that thinks that it's here and it has separated itself from its source and taken on an identity that is unique and personal. But even though it may look like there are billions of us here, there's really only one of us here and whatever you put out there is really just going to you. And not only that but your unconscious mind knowing anything knows that there's really only one of us here. And if your unconscious mind knows that there's really only one of us here, then it will interpret whatever you think about somebody else and whatever you say about somebody else to really be directed at you. So if you want to change your experience of life and ultimately your identity of what you are and what you think you are, then the fastest way to do it is to change the way you think about other people. ~ **Gary Renard**

Did you know there is an A Course in Miracles TV channel? Learn more at www.ACIMTVNETWORK.com

23

**"The Holy Spirit knows that you both *have* everything and *are* everything."** - *A Course in Miracles*

Day 5: Remember, The Course is but one theology that leads to God. What if this is a playground for God? What if you are God? How do these questions make you feel today? Do you become angry? Peaceful? Sad? Put pen to paper and discover for your true self. **-iKE**

_____

_____

_____

_____

_____

_____

_____

_____

_____

_____

_____

_____

_____

_____

*Our reality is an illusion, meaning the reality that we think is reality. Our true reality has nothing to do with what we're seeing, nothing to do with anything in this world. Our true reality is something that is whole and that is perfect. It's something that is immortal. It's invulnerable. It's something that actually can't be touched by anything in this world, it can't be threatened by anything in this world, and it goes on forever and that's the real us or the real you, because there's really only one of us, and that is spirit. But this idea of spirit is not the same as the way that the world traditionally thinks of spirit. The way that the world traditionally thinks of spirit is also a separation idea, it's kind of like an individual thing. It's like, I die and there's this part of me that goes on after me, after I die, and this thing that goes on after me, after I die, looks suspiciously like the body that I was just in. That's actually an idea of separation. That's not the kind of spirit that a great spiritual teaching like A Course in Miracles is talking about.* ~ **Gary Renard**

**"Ask for light and learn that you *are* light."**

*-A Course in Miracles*

Day 6: It's Day 6! I wanted to check in to see if you've had any experiences of actually scribing in your journal. If not, keep journaling and I invite you to also consider slowing down a bit when you put your pen on the page and see if Inspiration guides you. Gary's passage today is very challenging for many. Do you believe it to be true? Share your thoughts in your journal. -**iKE**

_____

_____

_____

_____

_____

_____

_____

_____

_____

_____

_____

Did you know there is an A Course in Miracles TV channel? Learn more at www.ACIMTVNETWORK.com

*One seeming paradox is, it's not happening, but you have the experience of it happening. You think it's happening. But when you have that total experience, then you realize this is all a dream, and it's not real. And that allows you then, in a sense, to return to the world and be totally free of any conflict, which means you could be totally present to anyone, anywhere, doing any activity, without any guilt, without any need, without any investment, and just be a totally loving presence. It's remarkably freeing.*

**~ Kenneth Wapnick**

**"Reality can dawn only on an unclouded mind."**

*-A Course in Miracles*

Day 7: When I first met Ken in Temecula, we had a playfully fun conversation in his office while we were alone. He looked at me and said, "Oh, you're like me." I coyly replied with, "Yes, but I have more hair." We then talked about what it was like to live in a world of sleeping giants and how seldom we each ran into other awakened people. We shared with each other about how we both felt compelled to help awaken others, not because there was actually anyone out there, but simply because it was our most natural expression. Spending time with Ken was like looking in a mirror. We both possessed the ongoing awareness of the Truth of who and what we really were. We both understood we were the same thing, having separate experiences. As Ken mentioned above, it is remarkably freeing. The conversation ended with Ken saying, "Okay, let's go back out there and play our roles." Ken and I had a wonderful experience where we both knew we were One. Today, journal about a moment in your life when you and another blended together into oneness. -iKE

_____

_____

_____

_____

_____

_____

_____

_____

_____

Did you know there is an A Course in Miracles TV channel? Learn more at www.ACIMTVNETWORK.com

# WEEK 2
## A Tiny Mad Idea

**The iKE ALLEN Tao Series**

*One of the terms The Course uses to describe the separation, or our belief in separation, is a "tiny mad idea." It's tiny because it's insignificant, meaning it had no effect, and it's mad because it's insane, and it's an idea because it's a thought. In other words, it's not anything that's in matter.*

## ~ Kenneth Wapnick

**"It is your thoughts alone that cause you pain."**

*-A Course in Miracles*

Day 8: Yesterday you journaled about a time when you and another blended into oneness. You have been one and you experience duality. Is it possible to return to Unity Consciousness *and* experience duality? Share your thoughts in your journal today.

**-iKE**

_____

_____

_____

_____

_____

_____

_____

_____

_____

_____

_____

_____

_____

Did you know there is an A Course in Miracles TV channel? Learn more at www.ACIMTVNETWORK.com

*In one place in the Teacher's Manual, it's talking about the separation. It says, "In time it happened long ago, in reality it never happened at all." And there's no way of accounting for it. If it never happened, what are we doing here? – which is a question that everyone raises, not only A Course in Miracles students, but in so many other spiritualities. How did all this happen? Especially when you deal with a non-dual thought system. It was a question that plagued, for example, Plotinus, who's perhaps the greatest Platonic philosopher, who followed Plato. And he had tremendous trouble. He was not a Christian, he did not believe in God, but he believed in the One, and that was his name for the Supreme Being in reality. And he struggled, as everyone does, with the idea "How could the One become many? How could this perfect One somehow end up here in the world?" And he never satisfactorily resolved it either.* ~ **Kenneth Wapnick**

**"The truth is simple; it is one without an opposite."**

*-A Course in Miracles*

Day 9: How could the One become many? We know what The Course says, but what thoughts or Inspirations come from inside you when you put pen to paper today? **-iKE**

_____

_____

_____

_____

_____

_____

_____

_____

_____

_____

_____

_____

_____

Did you know there is an A Course in Miracles TV channel? Learn more at www.ACIMTVNETWORK.com

*If you ask, even the question, "How could the tiny mad idea have arisen?" – you're saying it did arise and I want you to explain to me how it arose. So it's really a statement masquerading as a question. That argument comes in the Introduction to the Classification of Terms. So it's really not a question, it's a statement that says, "I believe the world is real, the separation is real and I want you to account for it." And anyone who is a damn fool enough to try to explain it is also falling into the trap of making it real.*

### ~ *Kenneth Wapnick*

33

**"What you think you are is a belief to be undone."**
*- A Course in Miracles*

Day 10: Was Buddha Enlightened? Did he experience being in this world but not of this world? The Course says, "a universal theology is impossible, but a universal experience is not only possible but necessary." I remember Ken telling me that most ACIM students forget the part of The Course that says, "It emphasizes application rather than theory, and experience rather than theology." Are you applying the principles of The Course in your life, or are you a person that simply talks about what The Course says? Today, journal about what my question brings up for you. Allow yourself to authentically share your feelings below. -iKE

_____

_____

_____

_____

_____

_____

_____

_____

_____

_____

_____

Did you know there is an A Course in Miracles TV channel? Learn more at www.ACIMTVNETWORK.com

*What Jesus then says, right after that passage is that, "Don't let theology delay you, seek only the experience." Don't try to understand what can't be understood. But when you have the experience of Love to which this Course leads you, within that experience of Love - which is non-dualistic, which is that of perfect Oneness - you will know that the tiny mad idea could never have happened and therefore it did not happen and then you wouldn't even ask the question.*

**~ Kenneth Wapnick**

**"Love is one. It has no separate parts and no degrees."**
*-A Course in Miracles*

Day 11: Again today, we're going to challenge you in regard to theology and specifically, *ACIM* theology. Are you able today to seek only the experience? If I tell you I am enlightened, what does this bring up for you? Are you able to remember perfect Oneness? Do you want to challenge my statement? What does The Course tell you to do? Share in your journal today. **-iKE**

_____

_____

_____

_____

_____

_____

_____

_____

_____

_____

_____

Did you know there is an A Course in Miracles TV channel? Learn more at www.ACIMTVNETWORK.com

*We believe there could be an opposite of the perfect Oneness that God created; there could be an opposite to the Self, the resplendent Self of Christ that God created – at One with himself. And that opposite, that self, is what the Ego becomes. That's what we think we are. And then we protect that self by making up a world that is itself an opposite of Heaven. So it's always a question of the opposite to what has no opposites.*

**~ Kenneth Wapnick**

**"Jesus became what all of you must be."**

*-A Course in Miracles*

Day 12: Mahatma Gandhi said, "Whatever you do will be insignificant, but it is very important that you do it." This is clearly another paradox that makes sense when we do not think, but *feel*. What do you feel today? Do you feel Holy Spirit wanting to speak through you in your journal today? Share your feelings. **-iKE**

_____

_____

_____

_____

_____

_____

_____

_____

_____

_____

_____

_____

_____

Did you know there is an A Course in Miracles TV channel? Learn more at www.ACIMTVNETWORK.com

*At the beginning of the Course, it says, "The opposite of Love is fear, but what is all encompassing can have no opposite," meaning there is no fear. "The opposite of Love is fear, but what is all encompassing can have no opposite." Which then means that fear does not exist; the Ego does not exist. So again, we come down to the same basic issue that our lives here on Earth are really meant to deny the Ego's denial of Truth – the denial of Truth meaning that separation is real, and we look at that in our own life by seeing ourselves as being separate from each other, otherwise that's not true.*

**~ *Kenneth Wapnick***

39

**"Perception is a choice and not a fact."**

-*A Course in Miracles*


Day 13: Do you have any fears today? In reading Ken's passage, do you see how you could let go of that fear? Today, allow Holy Spirit to guide you in your journaling and share what freedom from fear feels like for you. **-iKE**

_____

_____

_____

_____

_____

_____

_____

_____

_____

_____

_____

_____

Did you know there is an A Course in Miracles TV channel? Learn more at www.ACIMTVNETWORK.com

*Our bodies may be separate, but our Minds are all joined and are all the same.*

*~ **Kenneth Wapnick***

*"Do not see error.* **Do not make it real."**

*-A Course in Miracles*

Day 14: Plato said, "I am the wisest man alive, for I know one thing, and that is that I know nothing." What do you believe you know? When you return to Right Mind, what happens? Do you laugh? Cry? Rest? What do you then know? **-iKE**

_____

_____

_____

_____

_____

_____

_____

_____

_____

_____

_____

_____

_____

_____

Did you know there is an A Course in Miracles TV channel? Learn more at www.ACIMTVNETWORK.com

# WEEK 3
## Awaken Us From the Dream

**The iKE ALLEN Tao Series**

*There's a wonderful line saying that when you cross over to the real world, which is the Course's symbol for the end of the journey, you will realize "in glad astonishment that for all this, you gave up nothing." But on this side of the bridge, we're giving up everything. We're giving up not only what we cherish and what we love, but we're giving up our very self.*

**~ *Kenneth Wapnick***

**"The world you see does not exist."** -*A Course in Miracles*

Day 15: When you consider giving up your very self, what emotions do you feel? Today, journal about the emotions you're feeling while sitting with this. Do not think, simply put pen to paper and let the words flow, much like Helen did when she scribed The Course. **-iKE**

_____

_____

_____

_____

_____

_____

_____

_____

_____

_____

_____

_____

_____

_____

Did you know there is an A Course in Miracles TV channel? Learn more at www.ACIMTVNETWORK.com

*It is a trick question when you ask how did the illusion get created, because it never did, because it's just an illusion. It's kind of like when you're having a dream in bed at night - is the dream really there? I'm not here to say that events in a dream don't appear to happen. They do appear to happen but that doesn't mean they're real. It's like, let's say you peek in on your 3-year-old daughter, and she's having a bad dream - the kind we have in bed at night - and it seems real to her. What's happened is for all intents and purposes, that dream has become her reality. And she's tossing and turning, you can see she's uncomfortable and she's not having a good dream. So what do you do? You don't go over and shake the hell out of her because you don't want her to be afraid. So maybe instead you'll just whisper to her, you'll say things like "Hey it's only a dream, what you're seeing is not true." ~ **Gary Renard**

**"The world you see has nothing to do with reality."**
*-A Course in Miracles*

Day 16: Where are you in your journey today? Are you feeling fearful or anxious? Are you experiencing love and peace? Share your feelings again today. Put your pen to the journal below and witness what appears on the page as you open up to Holy Spirit. **-iKE**

_____

_____

_____

_____

_____

_____

_____

_____

_____

_____

_____

_____

_____

_____

_____

Did you know there is an A Course in Miracles TV channel? Learn more at www.ACIMTVNETWORK.com

*One of the things Helen Schucman, the Scribe of* A Course in Miracles *used to say, is that the Course is only for about five or six people. There was a period of time when she actually counted who she thought the five or six people were. I'm not going to give you the names. At some point, I think it was in a weak moment, she expanded it to nine or ten. But the point of that is not to take it as literally true, but as a symbol for the fact that this Course, in its pure form, in what it's really teaching, is for relatively few, because it's so frightening. It threatens the very fabric of our existence.*
**~ Kenneth Wapnick**

**"Your goal is to find out who you are."**

*-A Course in Miracles*

Day 17: Do you believe you truly want to awaken? Are you willing to remove all the blocks to love's presence? Today, Scribe/Journal about why you want the direct experience of Truth. Do you feel Holy Spirit helping you write in your journal today? -**iKE**

_____

_____

_____

_____

_____

_____

_____

_____

_____

_____

_____

_____

_____

_____

_____

Did you know there is an A Course in Miracles TV channel? Learn more at www.ACIMTVNETWORK.com

*If your happiness is dependent on what you're manifesting or making happen out there on the screen, you're in trouble, because it can't last. It is literally a world of shift and change and it's impermanent. So that's why people have never really been proven to be happy after they get what they want because it's not permanent. And the experience that we want to go for, is an experience that is permanent, that is there for you. An experience of peace that will last regardless of what appears to be happening out there on the screen, regardless of what you have or don't have or what you want or don't want. And that's true peace and that's true reality. That's the kind of thing that great masters like Buddha and Jesus were going for anyway, because they'd managed to shift from a condition of effect to being at cause of everything. And what that means is, a total idea, it's an idea where you eventually realize that the world is not being done to you. The world is actually being done by you. It's not coming at you, it's actually coming from you. It's kind of like a reversal of the way the world traditionally thinks. And when you go to a position of being a cause instead of effect, then you're no longer a victim. ~ **Gary Renard**

**"Can you imagine what a state of mind without illusions is?"**

*-A Course in Miracles*


Day 18: Gary's wisdom is profound today! Your world is coming from you! Where in your life today do you tell yourself that you're a victim? Place your pen on the page and share what you think Jesus would tell you in regard to thinking you're a victim. -**iKE**

_____

_____

_____

_____

_____

_____

_____

_____

_____

_____

_____

_____

Did you know there is an A Course in Miracles TV channel? Learn more at www.ACIMTVNETWORK.com

*If the world is being done to you then you're a victim. If the world was made by God, you'd be a victim. You'd be a victim of an outside force that was doing something to you. Then you're a victim, but as A Course in Miracles says: "I'm not a victim of the world I see." And when you start to realize that the world is being done by you, then forgiveness is justified. And as The Course says: "Anger is never justified." The Course doesn't say that you'll never get angry, but it does say anger is never justified. And the more you realize this and start to look at the world differently, then it becomes harder and harder to react to it. If you were in a movie theater and somebody up on the screen started yelling at you, you wouldn't take it very seriously. That's what this movie could be like, too. Somebody in the movie can start yelling at you and you kind of snicker and not take it seriously at all because there's nothing there to be taken seriously. ~ **Gary Renard***

**"Forget this world, forget this course...."**
*-A Course in Miracles*

Day 19: Walt Whitman said, "Do I contradict myself? Very well, then I contradict myself, I am large, I contain multitudes." Often, life appears to be a contradiction. We are here, we are not here. We should study this Course, we should forget this Course. What is a big contradiction in your life right now? Share it in your journal today.

**-iKE**

_____

_____

_____

_____

_____

_____

_____

_____

_____

_____

_____

_____

Did you know there is an A Course in Miracles TV channel? Learn more at www.ACIMTVNETWORK.com

*A common question that Course students ask is, (it's probably asked of many other spiritualities too, but certainly it's a commonly asked question in terms of A Course in Miracles) "Why do things seem to be getting worse instead of better? I'm such a serious, dedicated, sincere student. I've done the workbook 15 times already, I read the Text everyday, I just do everything I'm supposed to do and things are getting worse." Well it's not really that things are getting worse, things were already worse, but you never knew it. We are such good deniers. We are so well versed and expert at covering over our distress and projecting it out – and either covering it over by thinking the world is a good place, that the world makes us happy and gives us pleasure, it gives us joy, etc., or we cover it over by just attacking everybody and being angry all the time and blaming them for our problems – that we are not in touch with how awful we feel about ourselves and the rotten thought system we have all chosen to identify with. So things have already been bad. ~ **Kenneth Wapnick**

**"To mean you want the peace of God is to renounce all dreams."** *-A Course in Miracles*

Day 20: Today, ask Holy Spirit for guidance in choosing to see Truth. Put pen to paper and allow Holy Spirit to show you the way.
-iKE

_____

_____

_____

_____

_____

_____

_____

_____

_____

_____

_____

_____

_____

_____

Did you know there is an A Course in Miracles TV channel? Learn more at www.ACIMTVNETWORK.com

*What Jesus does for us in A Course in Miracles is, he lifts the veil so you can actually look within and see the cesspool of guilt and hate and pain that the Ego thought system is, that we have chosen to make our reality and to make our self. And as you work with this material more and more, and you recognize that you can't go for your special love relationships to make you happy, that you can no longer justify all your grievances and your hatreds, and attack thoughts of other people - everything gets brought back within to your Mind, and all of a sudden you realize what you have been doing. That's when the guilt begins to rise in your awareness. That's when things seem to be getting worse.* ~ **Kenneth Wapnick**

**"Heaven itself is reached with empty hands and open minds."** *-A Course in Miracles*

Day 21: Place your pen on the page and imagine one illusion of guilt you could let go of today. Scribe or journal about this today.
-iKE

_____

_____

_____

_____

_____

_____

_____

_____

_____

_____

_____

_____

_____

_____

Did you know there is an A Course in Miracles TV channel? Learn more at www.ACIMTVNETWORK.com

# WEEK 4
## Free Will

**The iKE ALLEN Tao Series** ☯

*We do have free will but it's not what people think. A Course in Miracles teaches that freedom of choice is your one remaining freedom as a prisoner of this world. You can decide to see it right. What that means is that you can change your interpretation of what you're seeing, you can choose to see it with the Holy Spirit instead of seeing it with the ego.*

**~ Gary Renard**

**"There is no road to travel on, and no time to travel through."** -*A Course in Miracles*

Day 22: Do you believe you have any free will? Perhaps you have the EXPERIENCE of free will and at the same time, it has already happened. How would this be possible? Share or scribe in your journal today. -**iKE**

_____

_____

_____

_____

_____

_____

_____

_____

_____

_____

_____

_____

_____

_____

Did you know there is an A Course in Miracles TV channel? Learn more at www.ACIMTVNETWORK.com

*You can choose to see people as being spirit instead of being a body. That's the one free will we have and everything else is just a smokescreen. It looks like there are a billion things out there to choose between, but there are really only two things to choose between, and only one of them is real. All you have is reality and unreality, and everything else is just bull. It's a trick to keep us looking out there on the screen because that's where the ego wants us to look, and if we do that, then we're really just fooling around with the screen.*

*~ **Gary Renard***

Did you know there is an A Course in Miracles TV channel? Learn more at www.ACIMTVNETWORK.com

**"The first step toward freedom involves a sorting out of the false from the true.**" -*A Course in Miracles*

Day 23: *A Course in Miracles* tells us that this world came and went long ago. My experience is that the story line of life appears to keep moving while my awareness continuously knows nothing is here. My life is much like a play. I say my lines as an actor and have no interest in rewriting them along the way. I enjoy the show as it rolls out. Do you truly want to be free? Are you willing to let go of your beliefs about free will? Your beliefs about Gary? Ken? Me? This book? Share or scribe authentically in your journal today. -iKE

_____

_____

_____

_____

_____

_____

_____

_____

_____

_____

*If I was at a movie theater and I wanted to change what was up there on the screen, it wouldn't do me much good to mess around with the screen. I might appear to change it temporarily but I'm not really changing the nature of it. If I want to change what was on that screen then I'd have to remember something. I'd have to remember that there's a projector, and that the projector is hidden. It's in the back of the theater. And if I really wanted to have a permanent impact on what's on that screen then I'd have to change what's in that projector. Only then would I be dealing with the cause instead of the effect. And there's an irony here, and the irony is that if you change the cause, then the effect would change anyway, it's just that that's no longer the focus.*
*~ **Gary Renard***

**"To learn this course requires willingness to question every value that you hold."** - *A Course in Miracles*

Day 24: Imagine how enjoyable life would be if you quit wasting your time trying to fix the screen in front of you. When you consider for a moment that you're the one projecting everything you see, there is an opportunity for peace. Today, share or scribe in your journal about what your life would be like if you consciously changed the film you were viewing. What new characters would you write into the story? Would they be helpful? Would they be loving?

-iKE

_____

_____

_____

_____

_____

_____

_____

_____

_____

_____

_____

Did you know there is an A Course in Miracles TV channel? Learn more at www.ACIMTVNETWORK.com

*Your focus needs to be on something that can work, something that can have a permanent and lasting impact instead of something that is only fleeting and temporary. That's the real remaining freedom that we have. What you would call free will is the decision to see it right. I'm not saying that there aren't amazing things that can happen as a result of that. Even though the script is written, as The Course teaches, which means it's already done, which would also go along with physics. Einstein said that past, present and future all occur simultaneously. Well if they all occurs simultaneously, then it would already be done, it's not like you're making it up as you go along. That's a false linear experience.*

**~ *Gary Renard***

Did you know there is an A Course in Miracles TV channel? Learn more at www.ACIMTVNETWORK.com

**"The Holy Spirit's Voice is as loud as your willingness to listen."** - *A Course in Miracles*

Day 25: The journey to enlightenment is a never ending paradox. Today, sit quietly for a few minutes and once you feel nudged to write about something, regardless of what it is, put pen to paper and share it in your journal. -iKE

_____

_____

_____

_____

_____

_____

_____

_____

_____

_____

_____

_____

Did you know there is an A Course in Miracles TV channel? Learn more at www.ACIMTVNETWORK.com

*The truth is holographic. The truth is, it's all already there. Now at the same time, there are, according to The Course, different dimensions of time. The Course teaches right in those first 50 miracles principles in the text, it says that the miracle works in all the dimensions of time. The miracle by the way, is forgiveness, but it's this unique kind of forgiveness that The Course is teaching, and it works in all the dimensions of time. What can happen as a result of doing this kind of forgiveness is that it's possible to actually switch dimensions of time. It's kind of like the principle of watching a DVD. You rent a DVD, sometimes it will have an alternate ending. And you can actually switch to the alternate ending and view a different scenario. Now it doesn't mean that you're making it up because that alternate ending has already been filmed, it's already there. It's just that now you're choosing to view something different, and that's all. ~ **Gary Renard***

**"Love is freedom."** -*A Course in Miracles*

Day 26: Where in your life are you feeling like you're a victim today? Have you ever felt victimized in this way before? If you're honest, you may notice a pattern in the ways you experience being unfairly treated. Today, I invite you to authentically say, "There must be another way. There must be another set of DVD's. There must be another way of looking at my life." Afterward, sit patiently with pen in hand and prepare to scribe a new outlook on life. If you are unable to authentically ask Holy Spirit for help, write your story about who is unfairly treating you and then, reread it 5 times in a row. Notice what happens as you reread it each time. (-: -**iKE**

_____

_____

_____

_____

_____

_____

_____

_____

_____

_____

_____

Did you know there is an A Course in Miracles TV channel? Learn more at www.ACIMTVNETWORK.com

*It's when you practice forgiveness, when you make that choice, that you open up the possibility of watching a different scenario, of watching a different ending on that DVD. But that's not our decision, that's the decision of the Holy Spirit. The reason for that is very simple. The Holy Spirit can see everything that ever happened from the beginning of time to the end of time. The Course teaches that the Holy Spirit looked back from the end of time and saw all the time held. So whose idea and judgment is going to be better? Yours or the Holy Spirit? Because the Holy Spirit can see everything, and all we're viewing is this tiny little speck of time and space which is itself just based on the idea of separation. If the Holy Spirit can see everything, it has to be the Holy Spirit's decision as to whether or not you change dimensions of time. The Holy Spirit guides us to what is best for everybody. I find that annoying, because I know what I want and I want it now, but maybe the Holy Spirit knows better. If you're doing this on your own and you're trying to manifest that mansion in Beverly Hills, well I'm sorry but maybe the Holy Spirit doesn't want you to have that mansion in Beverly Hills, because maybe that's not what's good for everybody. Because everything fits together, everything is one, everything is whole. A Course in Miracles talks about an interlocking chain of forgiveness. And so only the Holy Spirit can decide whether or not we should change dimensions of time. And at the same time, when you change dimensions, what the Holy Spirit does is erase that old dimension. It actually disappears from the hologram of time and space. ~ **Gary Renard***

Did you know there is an A Course in Miracles TV channel? Learn more at www.ACIMTVNETWORK.com

**"There is no substitute for peace."** - *A Course in Miracles*

Day 27: Make a miracle happen—give it every ounce of your love.
Journal about it and fill your page with agape. **-iKE**

_____

_____

_____

_____

_____

_____

_____

_____

_____

_____

_____

_____

_____

Did you know there is an A Course in Miracles TV channel? Learn more
at www.ACIMTVNETWORK.com

*The Course teaches that the Holy Spirit collapses time within the temporal sequence. So it's actually removing chunks of time as you go along practicing forgiveness. And your universe is disappearing around you and the Holy Spirit is taking your forgiveness and shining it through every dimension of time, every parallel universe, every past dream life or future dream life. It's shining it everywhere and we can't see that so we sit there and think, this is boring, nothing's happening. But the truth is, amazing things are happening and at the same time you're saving a great deal of time through this process of time collapse. In fact, The Course teaches that the miracle, which once again is forgiveness, can substitute for learning that may have taken thousands of years. So doing this kind of forgiveness can save you thousands of years, countless lifetimes, and accelerate your progress of spiritual growth dramatically. And the Holy Spirit is collapsing time and the universe is literally disappearing around you as the Holy Spirit does that.* ~ **Gary Renard**

**"Forgiveness is the end of specialness."**
*-A Course in Miracles*


Day 28: Are you ready to save thousands of years of watching reruns and eating stale popcorn? Are you ready to end your obsession with being special? Put pen to paper authentically. -iKE

_____

_____

_____

_____

_____

_____

_____

_____

_____

_____

_____

_____

Did you know there is an A Course in Miracles TV channel? Learn more at www.ACIMTVNETWORK.com

# WEEK 5

## Embracing True Forgiveness

**The iKE ALLEN Tao Series**

*Forgiveness in The Course is totally different from how it is usually thought of. Typically, when we think of forgiveness, we think that someone has done something to us, or those people with whom we identify, that requires us to forgive them their sin. The Course's position on forgiveness is that we forgive people for what they have not done, not for what they have done. Metaphysically, of course, what this means is that since there's no world and there's nothing here, there's nothing to forgive. But on a practical level, which is really the most important part of this Course – if you can't live this and demonstrate it, then it doesn't mean anything – on this level what it means is that what I forgive you for is that you have not taken God's love away from me.*
*~ **Kenneth Wapnick***

Did you know there is an A Course in Miracles TV channel? Learn more at www.ACIMTVNETWORK.com

**"Those you do not forgive you fear."** -*A Course in Miracles*

Day 29: Do you believe on the practical level that anyone here has taken God's love away from you? Think hard of everyone you've ever interacted with....ex spouses, ex lovers, ex friends, etc. Can you do something today to live and demonstrate forgiveness? Afterwards, journal about what happened. -**iKE**

_____

_____

_____

_____

_____

_____

_____

_____

_____

_____

_____

_____

_____

_____

Did you know there is an A Course in Miracles TV channel? Learn more at www.ACIMTVNETWORK.com

*The key element in all unforgiveness is that you have done something so reprehensible, so unconscionable, that nothing in the Universe could ever bring me to forgive you because of what you've done. Whether you've done it on a national scale, an international scale, or you've done it in my personal life. And all that I'm really doing is retaining a very shabby image of myself that says, "I am this worthless, vulnerable, helpless person, a victim of forces and powers and people beyond my control who can do with me what they will, and have the power to take my happiness away from me." And that's just a blatant lie. No one can take my happiness away from me except myself, because happiness is not found in the world, it's not found in my body getting its needs met, happiness is found in my choosing the teacher of happiness, which would be the Holy Spirit, or Jesus, who teach that sin and guilt are unreal – and that nothing has happened.*
~ ***Kenneth Wapnick***

**"Forgiveness, salvation, Atonement, true perception, all are one."** -*A Course in Miracles*

Day 30:  Do you still believe today that there are people that have done something so reprehensible, so unconscionable, that nothing in the universe could ever bring you to forgive them? It is very important to be honest about "what is." If you chose the teacher of happiness, would you be happy? Share in your journal. **-iKE**

_____

_____

_____

_____

_____

_____

_____

_____

_____

_____

_____

_____

_____

*Not one note in Heaven's Song is missed the Course says - that nothing happened to interfere with the perfect Love and the perfect Oneness of Heaven. Creator and created, cause and effect, Source and the effect of that Source have never been separated, so therefore, there's nothing to forgive. But we all accuse ourselves of having committed the unpardonable sin of separating from our Source. That's what we believe; and we built this whole world to protect us from the disastrous consequences of God's wrath that would come in our minds since that's where the sin occurred. So we make up the world of Body and seek to hide there, a world of mindlessness. And of course what this does is fulfill the Ego strategy that "if I don't know I have a Mind, how can I change my Mind and choose the Holy Spirit as my teacher?" So the Ego makes up a world and makes up a separate body into which we think we were born, and that makes us mindless. Again, I can't change a Mind I don't know I have. So what I then do is I take the sin I believe I've committed, I project it out onto other people and blame them. ~ **Kenneth Wapnick***

**"Only in someone else can you forgive yourself...."**
*-A Course in Miracles*

Day 31: Imagine being constantly aware that you never separated and yet, you're still having this experience on this planet called Earth. How would your life look and feel without guilt and shame? Put pen to paper and paint a picture of your life when filled with love. **-iKE**

_____

_____

_____

_____

_____

_____

_____

_____

_____

_____

_____

_____

Did you know there is an A Course in Miracles TV channel? Learn more at www.ACIMTVNETWORK.com

*What has to be forgiven is not what the world has done to me; what has to be forgiven is what I believe I did to the world. I chose to make other people sinful, and guilty and responsible for my own secret sin, that I'm the one who separated from God's love. And so, I forgive you for what you have not done, because regardless of what you may have done with your Body to my Body, you have not had any effect on my Mind. And so, forgiveness then means, simply, that I return to my Mind, I recall the projections of my guilt that I put onto you, I bring the guilt back within, and then I recognize that guilt is also something that I made. Not only did I make up my anger at you, but I made up my own guilt, because there was no separation, nothing happened. The Holy Spirit is the great principle of the "nothing happened." That's what the Course calls the Principle of the Atonement – nothing happened, there was no separation. And if nothing happened, there was no sin. And if I did not sin, there's nothing to project.*
*~ **Kenneth Wapnick***

Did you know there is an A Course in Miracles TV channel? Learn more at www.ACIMTVNETWORK.com

**Freedom from illusions lies only in not believing them**."

*- A Course in Miracles*

Day 32: If you truly wish to awaken, you must forgive yourself for something you did not do, and on the practical level, you must forgive anyone that you have projected guilt onto. Do you really want to awaken? Have you truly forgiven yourself and everyone in your life? **-iKE**

_____

_____

_____

_____

_____

_____

_____

_____

_____

_____

_____

_____

_____

Did you know there is an A Course in Miracles TV channel? Learn more at www.ACIMTVNETWORK.com

*When I forgive, I basically am applying what the Course calls the three steps of forgiveness. It doesn't call it that, but it enumerates three steps. The first step says, "You are not the source of my problem." Because the guilt is not in you, it's in me. Again, regardless of what you've done, your Ego is your problem but it's not my problem. I bring the guilt that I projected onto you back to my own Mind, and the second step, I look at the guilt in my Mind and I realize that I've chosen it! And because I chose it, I can choose against it. And that's it, I'm done, because the third step, the Course says, is the Holy Spirit always, he just takes the guilt away. And it's not that he literally takes it away; what happens is that when I change my Mind about it, it disappears. And by realizing that I chose the wrong teacher, and I see the disastrous consequences of that mistaken choice, I'm automatically going to choose the correct one. ~ **Kenneth Wapnick***

**"That there is choice is an illusion."** -*A Course in Miracles*

Day 33: Today, bring the guilt you've projected onto others back to your own mind. Journal about it in your own mind and share your thoughts on choosing against it. **-iKE**

_____

_____

_____

_____

_____

_____

_____

_____

_____

_____

_____

_____

_____

_____

*There's a line in the Text that says, "Who, with the love of God upholding him, will find the choice between miracles and murder hard to make?" "Who with the love of God upholding him," which occurs when we become Right-Minded, "will find the choice between miracles and murder hard to make?" All forgiveness does, all the Miracle does, which is why the book is called* A Course in Miracles, *is bring the problem from the dream, from the world and Body back to the Mind, so I can realize I made a mistaken choice, I can make a better one, and that's it. I will automatically choose the right teacher, a teacher that will lead me to this quiet joy, this peace that just permeates everything and a peace and a joy that embraces everyone without exception. That's how forgiveness works. ~ **Kenneth Wapnick***

**"The dreamer of a dream is not awake, but does not know he sleeps."** -*A Course in Miracles*

Day 34: What better choice could you make today if you brought a perceived problem from the dream, back to the mind? Share or scribe in your journal today. **-iKE**

_____

_____

_____

_____

_____

_____

_____

_____

_____

_____

_____

_____

_____

_____

_____

Did you know there is an A Course in Miracles TV channel? Learn more at www.ACIMTVNETWORK.com

*As you're practicing forgiveness you're having the guilt in your mind healed by the Holy Spirit. You enjoy life more when this happens. A lot of people think it's about giving up things in this world. I contend that you can enjoy this world more, not less if you practice this kind of forgiveness, because you'll have less guilt in your mind. If you have less guilt in your mind, you'll feel better, enjoy things more, enjoy sex more, enjoy the things you have in this life even more. It's like when I go to a movie, which is my hobby, I know that it's not real. But that doesn't stop me from enjoying it. That's what this movie can be like too. I'll say you can enjoy it more. I'm not into giving up having romantic walks on the beach, the beautiful sunsets and the lovely arts and music. It's not really about giving up those things, it's simply about changing your experience back to what you really are, about achieving a higher identity, a higher life form. And it really is a better life form, it really is a better way of life, and that's why you should do it. That's why I practice forgiveness. If I forgive I know that I'll feel better, I know that it'll make a difference for me, I know that I will be healed and that I'm going home. ~ **Gary Renard***

**"There is a place in you where there is perfect peace.**
*-A Course in Miracles*


Day 35: When you forgive, do you feel better? If you do, why do you still hold grudges? What story of betrayal could you let go of today? Journal about the betrayal and then, read what you wrote at least 3 times. What happens? Share authentically. -iKE

_____

_____

_____

_____

_____

_____

_____

_____

_____

_____

_____

_____

_____

_____

Did you know there is an A Course in Miracles TV channel? Learn more at www.ACIMTVNETWORK.com

# WEEK 6
## Why Do We Suffer?

**The iKE ALLEN Tao Series**

*We are responsible for the world's suffering. God has absolutely nothing to do with it. God has nothing to do with this world and we should be happy about that because if God had anything to do with it, then he'd be just as crazy as we are. And then we would not have a perfect God to go home to. We would not have a perfect kingdom of heaven to return home to. So God does not interact with this world, has nothing to do with it, is totally sane, and that absolves God of responsibility. In fact I think that the God of A Course in Miracles really is perfect love.*

*~ Gary Renard*

Did you know there is an A Course in Miracles TV channel? Learn more at www.ACIMTVNETWORK.com

85

**"The special love relationship is an attempt to bring love into separation."** -*A Course in Miracles*

Day 36: Today, I'm throwing you a curve-ball. Simply make a list of every past romantic relationship and every friendship you have ever had that ended badly. That's it! -**iKE**

_____

_____

_____

_____

_____

_____

_____

_____

_____

_____

_____

_____

_____

_____

_____

_____

Did you know there is an A Course in Miracles TV channel? Learn more at www.ACIMTVNETWORK.com

*A lot of things like the Bible have said that God is love and that God is perfect love. Then they go on to resent us with their behavior and with their scripture with a God who is anything but perfect love. A Course in Miracles on the other hand gives us a God that really is perfect, that really is flawless and eternal. And the word eternal means without time. I used to think of it as a linear thing that goes on forever, but it's an experience without time. In this experience there is no next. In this world, there's always a next. I got the job, what's next? I got the girl, what's next? I got my degree, what's next? There's always a next because that's there to have something to go for. It's like a carrot and a stick that will hope that you're going to fulfill this imaginary lack that wouldn't even exist if you could rejoin with God.*

**~ Gary Renard**

**"The world you see is the delusional system of those made mad by guilt."** -*A Course in Miracles*

Day 37: Today, look at the list you made yesterday. Next to each person's name, list whose fault it was that the relationship ended - yours or theirs. **-iKE**

_____

_____

_____

_____

_____

_____

_____

_____

_____

_____

_____

_____

_____

_____

_____

_____

Did you know there is an A Course in Miracles TV channel? Learn more at www.ACIMTVNETWORK.com

*A Course in Miracles says that the only problem is the idea that we have separated ourselves from our source and taken on an individual existence and identity that is separate from our source. Practicing A Course in Miracles undoes that idea much like the concept of undoing the ego in Buddhism. And by undoing, eventually the real you will be all that's left. So the focus of The Course isn't on trying to perfect that which is already perfect. The focus of The Course is on trying to undo that which is not perfect, and if you do that, then eventually the real you is all that's left. And that's actually the Hindu and Buddhist concept of undoing the ego. Except The Course does it a little bit differently. It does it by changing the way you look at others and yourself. You can forgive yourself just as easily as others, it doesn't matter, because there's no difference between forgiving this part of the projection and the other part of the projection.*

**~ *Gary Renard***

**"Love and guilt cannot coexist, and to accept one is to deny the other."** *-A Course in Miracles*

Day 38: If noBODY else is a sinner, are you? If noBODY else is even here, are you? Perhaps you are still safely at home? I believe you are. Journal your thoughts and have a wonderFULL day. **-iKE**

_____

_____

_____

_____

_____

_____

_____

_____

_____

_____

_____

_____

_____

Did you know there is an A Course in Miracles TV channel? Learn more at www.ACIMTVNETWORK.com

*If I hold my hand up in front of my face, what is that? It's really just a part of the same projection as everything else is. It's not really separate from that. I used to think that this body was very important because it was the closest one to me. So I figured that must be me. But it's not, it's really just a part of the same projection as everything else. And we think that we're seeing what we're seeing through the body's eyes, but we're not. The idea of having a body and having eyes is a part of that same projection as everything else, and what we're really doing is reviewing mentally that which has already gone by. And that's very much the same concept as watching a movie, because the movie has already been filmed. And we sit there and we watch it and pretend that it never happened before and that we're making it up as we're going along. That's a linear experience. And that's what most spiritualities are based on. I'm going to use my thoughts to make this happen or that happen, I'm going to manifest the Mercedes, I'm going to manifest the mansion in Beverly hills. And if you do that, I'm not saying that there's anything wrong with that, I'm just saying that if you do that, it's not addressing the one real problem. It's kind of like moving around the furniture in a burning house. Yeah, you might make it look better for awhile, but it's ignoring the real problem. ~ **Gary Renard***

Did you know there is an A Course in Miracles TV channel? Learn more at www.ACIMTVNETWORK.com

**"Guilt feelings are the preservers of time."**

*-A Course in Miracles*


Day 39: Who are you still secretly hating? Look deep within and journal today about why you hate them. After you are done, reread what you wrote 10 times in a row. How do you feel afterward? Why? -iKE

_____

_____

_____

_____

_____

_____

_____

_____

_____

_____

_____

_____

_____

Did you know there is an A Course in Miracles TV channel? Learn more at www.ACIMTVNETWORK.com

*The real problem is that the house is burning down and you have to address the real problem. Moving around the furniture ain't gonna do you too much good. I'm not saying you can't do that, it's like Jesus would say: "Yeah, you can use the power of the mind to have anything you want. You can move mountains. But where you gonna put them?" After awhile it's just stuff. As Kevin Spacey said in* American Beauty. *He's having an argument with his wife because she's into all the furniture. And he looks at her and says: "It's just stuff!" And that's all it is. It's nothing, absolutely nothing. But when we become attached to it and think it's important, all we're really doing is setting ourselves up for that time when it won't be there. The ego loves it because the ego wants to keep us looking out there on the screen where the answer isn't, which is the effect, instead of looking within to the cause, which is the mind, where the answer really is. And so one of the ways the ego accomplishes this, is that it made the body. The body is a real piece of work because it allows into awareness only that which conforms to the reality of the ego's cherished illusions. It's kind of like a multi-sensory movie and seems so real. And then to top it off - and this is really devious - to top it off, I am born as the perfect little victim. I'm an innocent little baby, I'm helpless. How can I possibly have had anything to do with this world, how can I possibly have had anything to do with making this? Here I am this innocent little victim and I was made by other bodies and it's not my fault, my parents did it. It's their fault and not only that, you know what? They didn't love me enough. ~ **Gary Renard**

Did you know there is an A Course in Miracles TV channel? Learn more at www.ACIMTVNETWORK.com

93

**"When you look into an abyss, the abyss also looks into you."** *-Friedrich Nietzsche*

Day 40: Today, look deep within for the answer to all your suffering. Today, you have the chance to actually face it. Will you take the Leap!? **-iKE**

_____

_____

_____

_____

_____

_____

_____

_____

_____

_____

_____

_____

_____

_____

Did you know there is an A Course in Miracles TV channel? Learn more at www.ACIMTVNETWORK.com

*If you think they're a body, it's going to mean that you'll think you're a body and everything you ever did, every little word you said to somebody in your whole life and every lifetime really happened. But on the other hand, if they're innocent, that means that you're innocent. If they're not a body and are spirit, and they're all of it, that means you're spirit and you're all of it. But to do that and to experience it you have to see everybody that your eyes appear to see as completely innocent. The way Jesus puts it in A Course in Miracles, he says: "Innocence is not a partial attribute. It's not until it becomes a viewpoint with universal application that it becomes wisdom." So there you see Jesus' definition of wisdom is a little different then the world's idea of wisdom. The world's idea of wisdom is that you have good judgment. But Jesus' idea of wisdom would be that you saw everybody as being completely innocent and left nobody out, because that's the only way to truly have it for yourself. Now if you partially forgive the world, like most people, then you will experience yourself as being partially forgiven. And you will not be enlightened and will not return to your source.*

**~ *Gary Renard***

**"You are not the victim of the world you see because you invented it.** *" -A Course in Miracles*

Day 41: Today, who will you forgive for something they have not done to you? This is where we push deeper. Use your journal for support and accelerated freedom. -**iKE**

_____

_____

_____

_____

_____

_____

_____

_____

_____

_____

_____

_____

_____

Did you know there is an A Course in Miracles TV channel? Learn more at www.ACIMTVNETWORK.com

*It's only when you completely forgive the world the way Jesus did - which means he forgave every memory in his mind, and what is a memory except a picture in the mind? Which means that you can forgive anything that ever happened to you in your life. Even if something terrible happened to you when you were a child, maybe you were abused or something, you can forgive that because that's a picture in the mind, and what's this that we're seeing right now except a picture in the mind? So you can forgive anything, every memory, every relationship, every event that you see on tv, every situation you feel stuck in, every relationship you feel bad about, you can forgive it and use it for the Holy Spirit's purposes, which is to return to wholeness, to oneness. And when you do that, you're doing something that very few people in history have ever done. But in order to do it you have to realize that no room for compromise is possible in this. If you withhold your love and your forgiveness from anybody, then it is not real love and forgiveness. It's an artificial kind of love and forgiveness that just keeps you stuck here. It's only when you realize that it has to be for everyone in order for it to be completely for you, that it becomes wisdom and then you can use these ideas to undo the ego and to go home.* ~ **Gary Renard**

Did you know there is an A Course in Miracles TV channel? Learn more at www.ACIMTVNETWORK.com

**"It is your thoughts alone that cause you pain."**
*- A Course in Miracles*

Day 42: Do you still believe you need to be punished in some way? Today, share about this in your journal and then, turn it over to Holy Spirit. **-iKE**

_____

_____

_____

_____

_____

_____

_____

_____

_____

_____

_____

_____

_____

_____

_____

_____

Did you know there is an A Course in Miracles TV channel? Learn more at www.ACIMTVNETWORK.com

# WEEK 7

## God's Perfect Oneness

**The iKE ALLEN Tao Series**

*When we address the question, "Is it worthwhile to become a better person, or to do good works in the world and help people?" – in order to answer that, we need a little background in terms of the Course, and that is to understand the crucial distinction the Course makes between the Body and the Mind. The Body is the part of our self, obviously, that we identify with, and I think one could understand in the Course that the word Body not only includes our physical body but our psychological body – in other words, our personalities, our emotions, etc. And the Course is quite adamant that the Body does absolutely nothing. There are many, many, many passages, in all three books, the Text, Workbook and Teacher's Manual, that say things like: "The Body is not born. It does not die. It doesn't get sick. It doesn't get well. It doesn't attack. It can't be attacked. Eyes don't see. Ears don't hear. Brains don't think. Bodies don't decide." And on and on and on.* ~ **Kenneth Wapnick**

**"Health is the result of relinquishing all attempts to use the body lovelessly."** *-A Course in Miracles*

Day 43: Thoughts? **-iKE**

_____

_____

_____

_____

_____

_____

_____

_____

_____

_____

_____

_____

_____

_____

_____

Did you know there is an A Course in Miracles TV channel? Learn more at www.ACIMTVNETWORK.com

*Everything is done, in what the Course calls, the Mind. And it's very important when one talks about the Mind, from the perspective of the Course, that one understands that the Mind is not the brain. Very, very often, when brain/mind researchers do their work and write their books, they really use the Mind in some way as being kind of an extension of the brain, that the brain is a physical organ and the Mind is the activity of the brain that can't be studied. But that's not the position of the Course. The Course says very clearly that the Mind is not in the Body; the Body is in the Mind. In other words, that what we think, as a projection of the Mind's thought system, is a Body, and that, in the cosmological sense as the physical Universe, it has never left its source. And that would seem to be outside if you're inside, and what we think is outside is simply an hallucination, which is the term the Course actually uses.*

**~ *Kenneth Wapnick***

**"All are called but few choose to listen."**
*-A Course in Miracles*

Day 44: The body is in the mind. You are safely at home and you're still having the experience of this life. If someone needs help, what is the loving thing to do? Who could you help today? **-iKE**

_____

_____

_____

_____

_____

_____

_____

_____

_____

_____

_____

_____

_____

_____

_____

Did you know there is an A Course in Miracles TV channel? Learn more at www.ACIMTVNETWORK.com

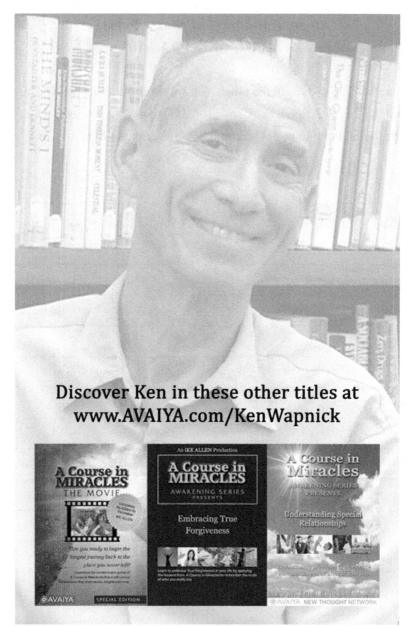

Discover Ken in these other titles at
www.AVAIYA.com/KenWapnick

Did you know there is an A Course in Miracles TV channel? Learn more at www.ACIMTVNETWORK.com

Did you know there is an A Course in Miracles TV channel? Learn more at www.ACIMTVNETWORK.com

*When we talk about doing things in the world, the question is, "What is doing the things?" There's a rhetorical question early on in the Text that says, "Who is the you who are living in this world?" "Who is the 'you' who are living in this world?" And the answer is that it's not the Body. It's the Mind that thinks it's in the world. And actually, our True Self, which is the ultimate subject of that passage, is actually Self as Christ, as Spirit, which is not in this world at all. But the Mind is where all the activity is; it's the Mind that held the thought – what the Course calls the tiny mad idea – that believes that we can be separate from our Creator and Source, and set up a self that's the opposite of this glorious capital S Self that God created. That we set up a world that's the opposite of Heaven, a place where everything changes, differences abound, and everything in the end, dies – animate or inanimate. It may take millions of years for a rock to deteriorate and disappear, but it will. Heaven is changeless and is eternal. And then when we believe we separated – that's what occurred in the Mind, the split Mind or the separated Mind – that's the actor, that's where the decisions are made, that's where we always are, though we are dreaming.* ~ ***Kenneth Wapnick***

**"All your time is spent in dreaming."** *-A Course in Miracles*

Day 45: Buddha said, "The mind is everything. What you think you become." Who are you today? Who will you be tomorrow? **-iKE**

_____

_____

_____

_____

_____

_____

_____

_____

_____

_____

_____

_____

_____

_____

_____

_____

Did you know there is an A Course in Miracles TV channel? Learn more at www.ACIMTVNETWORK.com

*When we are asleep at night having a dream, we are asleep in our bed and our dream takes us to all kinds of places in the world and all kinds of fanciful, impossible things happen and yet, we never leave our bed, never! – unless we're sleepwalkers I guess, but typically we don't leave our bed - and so while we are asleep, we think we are in these exotic places doing these exotic things or terrible things. Our body reacts physiologically as if things were being done to us. Yet we open our eyes and awaken and say, "Thank God it was only a dream!" and we realize there's nobody with us and we're still in our bed. Nothing's happened.*
*~ **Kenneth Wapnick***

**"You are the dreamer of the world of dreams."**
*-A Course in Miracles*

Day 46: When you let go of the idea that you're actually here, the awareness that you're safely at home returns. Are you ready to hold onto this awareness as you walk within the dream? Share your thoughts why or why not in your journal today. **-iKE**

_____

_____

_____

_____

_____

_____

_____

_____

_____

_____

_____

_____

_____

_____

_____

Did you know there is an A Course in Miracles TV channel? Learn more at www.ACIMTVNETWORK.com

*Jesus teaches us in A Course in Miracles that nothing has happened; we just are dreaming that we are here. Dreaming that our body is doing things, dreaming that we are becoming a better person. Dreaming that we are doing great and wonderful things in the world, like teaching A Course in Miracles, which is a joke. Whom are you teaching, and who is doing the teaching? If there's nobody out here 'cause there's no world, we are simply teaching ourselves. And when we talk about forgiveness and relationships, it's extraordinarily important, as a student of the Course, that you realize, even though the language of the Course is dualistic, and the language of the Course meets us on the level of our experience - same way as bodies - what the Course is really teaching us is that I don't forgive somebody else. I don't forgive my mother or my father or my friends or my children or my spouses or my employers or my President or Prime Minister; I forgive myself. There's no one out there!* ~ **Kenneth Wapnick**

**"Dreams disappear when light has come and you can see."**
*-A Course in Miracles*

Day 47: Even as one awakens, the dreamland continues. Ken and I both realized there is no one actually reading these pages, and yet, Ken continued teaching until his apparent death, and I, too, continue teaching, creating films and books and more. I fully realize I am always teaching myself, reminding myself about the Truth. Today, I invite you to live your life as if you're an actor playing a role. Tonight, share in your journal about your experience. **-iKE**

_____

_____

_____

_____

_____

_____

_____

_____

_____

_____

_____

_____

Did you know there is an A Course in Miracles TV channel? Learn more at www.ACIMTVNETWORK.com

*When I forgive, it's when I basically fire the Ego as my teacher saying, "I no longer want to learn from you." I now choose a different teacher – the Holy Spirit or Jesus – that's my holy relationship. I always counsel students, "Run away as fast as you can from someone who says to you, 'I and this other person have a holy relationship.'" Because that means they're making the Body real and they think they're special. The only holy relationship there is, is between your decision making Mind and the Holy Spirit. And when that relationship is chosen, all your relationships become holy, because there's nothing out here. When you choose your Ego as your teacher, all of your relationships become special because there's no one out here. That's what the Course means when it says, "When you forgive one person, you've forgiven all of them." When you totally forgive one person, you've forgiven all of them. It says, "Behind this one person, stands thousands more and behind each one stand another thousand." Of course, it's all One. It's my guilt that I project out and it permeates and contaminates every relationship I had, even when I'm not aware of it. But when I choose to forgive, and let go of the guilt, which means I let go of my belief in separation, that you and I are separate, then all my relationships become holy. Even with people I haven't even met yet. ~ **Kenneth Wapnick***

**"An unholy relationship is no relationship."**
*-A Course in Miracles*

Day 48: Have you truly forgiven yourself for the illusion of separation? Journal today about why or why not. **-iKE**

_____

_____

_____

_____

_____

_____

_____

_____

_____

_____

_____

_____

_____

_____

_____

_____

Did you know there is an A Course in Miracles TV channel? Learn more at www.ACIMTVNETWORK.com

*If you really knew and believed the world were an illusion, you would not see anyone as separate. Because what "the world is an illusion" means is that God's reality of perfect Oneness is the Truth, which means everyone here is part of that Oneness. When you are totally Right-Minded, which really comes from that understanding and appreciation that the world is an illusion and the only reality is the Non-Dual reality, there's only Spirit and Truth and nothing else. Then everything you do will come from that place of Truth in your Mind and it will be totally loving and will not exclude anyone, but embrace everyone.*
*~ **Kenneth Wapnick***

**"It is impossible to overestimate your brother's value."**

*- A Course in Miracles*

Day 49: Today, I invite you to share how much you love everyone. Facebook, Twitter, email, phone calls, etc. Spend part of your day letting everyone here that is part of the Oneness, know you love them. In your journal, perhaps simply draw a smiley face. I LOVE YOU! -iKE (-:

_____

_____

_____

_____

_____

_____

_____

_____

_____

_____

_____

_____

Did you know there is an A Course in Miracles TV channel? Learn more at www.ACIMTVNETWORK.com

In addition, congratulate yourSELF as this is your final day. I hope you have had a joyful journey with Kenneth Wapnick and Gary Renard.

**Spend more time with Kenneth Wapnick at:**

www.KennethWapnick.com

**Spend more time with Gary Renard at:**

www.avaiya.com/Gary

Did you know there is an A Course in Miracles TV channel? Learn more at www.ACIMTVNETWORK.com

# ABOUT THE AUTHOR

**iKE ALLEN** is an internationally sought after speaker and the founder of AVAIYA (www.AVAIYA.com). AVAIYA creates positive media such as *The Tao Of* book series, and the films *A Course in Miracles The Movie, Remembering Kenneth Wapnick,* and the *ACIM Awakening Series Courses.* For speaking engagements, seminars or to host iKE for his ACIM interactive presentation featuring rare footage with several ACIM Teachers, visit www.iKEALLEN.com. iKE's ultimate passion is experiencing the joys and challenges of raising two gorgeous daughters to live a life of true power, fun, and exploration.

Did you know there is an A Course in Miracles TV channel? Learn more at www.ACIMTVNETWORK.com

# NOTES

Did you know there is an A Course in Miracles TV channel? Learn more
at www.ACIMTVNETWORK.com

# NOTES

Did you know there is an A Course in Miracles TV channel? Learn more at www.ACIMTVNETWORK.com

# NOTES

Did you know there is an A Course in Miracles TV channel? Learn more at www.ACIMTVNETWORK.com

# NOTES

Did you know there is an A Course in Miracles TV channel? Learn more at www.ACIMTVNETWORK.com

# NOTES

Made in the USA
Las Vegas, NV
06 April 2021